Vancouver's Endearing Splendour of Flowers Collection 2024

Rowena Kong

Annie Ho

Ronnie Kong

Rowena Kong
2024

First Printing: 2024

ISBN: 978-1-998518-02-9

The Royal Bonica rose, a long-standing beauty of resilience and grace, shines strong through summer and autumn…

Introduction

Located on the western end of the lower mainland of British Columbia in Canada, Vancouver is a city blessed with one of the mildest weather conditions in the country befitting for a variety of blossoms through the seasons of the year. From late winter's Primrose to autumn's Aster, there is a wide range of flower genus to choose from for one's gardening pleasure. This guide serves as a convenient alphabetical listing of both the more popular and lesser known flower varieties which one can find available in garden centres as well as featured in public parks within nature-loving Vancouver.

1.African Daisy (Osteospermum)
Colour: White; Purple; Pink; Yellow
First Bloom: April
Scent: None
Petal Size: Medium

African daisies, with their rich colours, do well too in partial sun and shady spots. They can be planted in pots and add a stunning view to your windowsills. The deep hues of their flower centres provide captivating contrast to their petals, making them great candidates for displays and photoshoots.

2. Allium "Onion Flower"
   Colour: Purple; Violet
   First Bloom: April
   Scent: None
   Petal Size: Tiny

3.Alyssum (Lobularia maritima)
Colour: White; Purple; Green
First Bloom: April
Scent: Strong
Petal Size: Small

4.Aster (Aster)
Colour: Purple; Orange
First Bloom: September
Scent: Mild
Petal Size: Medium

Aster is particularly attractive to bees in autumn during its full bloom, when these helpers of pollination get to work with brimming enthusiasm.

5.Baby Blue Eyes (Nemophila menziesii)
Colour: Blue; White
First Bloom: June
Amount of Sun Needed: Moderate to Full
Scent: None
Petal Size: Small

These delightful baby blues will cast a sea of joy as a ground cover and along hedges, wonder to behold and adore for their twinkling sight and innocent beauty.

6.Bacopa (Bacopa monnieri)
    Colour: White; Yellow
    First Bloom: April
    Amount of Sun Needed: Moderate to Full
    Scent: None
    Petal Size: Considerably Small

7.Bluebell (Hyacinthoides non-scripta)
    Colour: Blue; Purple; Violet
    First Bloom: March to April
    Amount of Sun Needed: Mild
    Scent: None
    Petal Size: Fairly Small
    Heralding early spring, bluebells burst forth in abundance in the fields and shady grounds, bringing sweet charm and adorable cover over greens with their childlike flower beauty that touches one's heart.

8.Bonica Rose (Rosa 'Bonica 82')
Colour: Pink; White
First Bloom: June
Amount of Sun Needed: Moderate to Full
Scent: None
Petal Size: Medium

9.Calendula (Calendula officinalis)
   Colour: Yellow; Orange
   First Bloom: June to July
   Amount of Sun Needed: Moderate to Full
   Scent: None
   Petal Size: Fairly Medium
Calendula blooms as early as late June and as pictured below, resembles daisy-like slender petals with delicate splits and cute deeper tone centres. They are a lively ground garden addition, giving a touch of summer brightness and colour cheer.

10.California Poppy (Eschscholzia californica)
   Colour: Golden Yellow; Orange
   First Bloom: June
   Amount of Sun Needed: Moderate to Full
   Scent: None
   Petal Size: Medium

Adding a splash of golden yellows and oranges to this lawn,
California poppies bloom with welcoming cheer and bliss for any
garden visitor.

11. Candytuft (Iberis)
Colour: Purple; Violet: White; Pink; Yellow; Varied
First Bloom: July
Amount of Sun Needed: Mild to Moderate
Scent: None
Petal Size: Small

12. "Caramel Fairytale" Rose by Floribunda(Rosa)
Colour: Caramel-like; Yellowish Orange
First Bloom: June
Amount of Sun Needed: Moderate to Full
Scent: None
Petal Size: Medium

13. Carnation (Dianthus caryophyllus)
    Colour: Pink; Red; White
    First Bloom: March
    Amount of Sun Needed: Full
    Scent: None
    Petal Size: Small to Fairly Medium

14.Cherry Blossom (Prunus serrulata)
Colour: Pink; White
First Bloom: Mid-March
Amount of Sun Needed: Moderate
Scent: Mild
Petal Size: Small to Large

"Akebono"

"Kanzan"

"Ukon"

15. Columbine/Granny's Bonnet (Aquilegia)
    Colour: Blue; Purple; Violet; Varied
    First Bloom: May
    Amount of Sun Needed: Mild to Moderate
    Scent: None
    Petal Size: Medium

The Columbine flower is unique in its double layer of contrasting petal shapes, with rounded edged ones over those sharp and narrow ended, a well-blended combination that showcases diversity of nature…

16.Cosmos (Cosmos bipinnatus)
Colour: Pink; Light Purple; Red; White; Yellow
First Bloom: May
Scent: None
Petal Size: Medium

17.Crocus (Crocus tommasinianus)
Colour: White; Purple; Violet; Yellow; Orange(Stamen)
First Bloom: March
Amount of Sun Needed: Moderate
Scent: None
Petal Size: Medium

18.Daffodil (Narcissus)
Colour: Yellow; Orange; White
First Bloom: Early April
Amount of Sun Needed: Moderate
Scent: None
Petal Size: Medium

19. Dahlia (Dahlia hortensis)
    Colour: Purple; Pink; White; Variety
    First Bloom: August
    Scent: None
    Petal Size: Small(Multi-Layered)
Dahlia can grow as tall as close to a metre towards late summer, boasting a variety of eye-catching shades and thrive in bushy groups.

20.Dogwood (Cornus florida)
Colour: Pink; White; Green
First Bloom: June
Scent: None
Petal Size: Medium

21.Forget-Me-Not (Myosotis)
    Colour: Blue; Pink; Purple; White; Yellow
    First Bloom: Mid-April
    Amount of Sun Needed: Moderate
    Scent: None
    Petal Size: Small

22.French Hollyhock (Malva sylvestris)
Colour: Purple; Blue; White; Violet; Varied
First Bloom: May
Amount of Sun Needed: Mild
Scent: None
Petal Size: Fairly Medium

23."Garden Delight" Rose by Floribunda(Rosa)
Colour: Pink; Peach; Red; White; Yellow; Orange; Varied
First Bloom: June
Amount of Sun Needed: Moderate to Full
Scent: None
Petal Size: Medium to Fairly Large

24.Geranium (Pelargonium)
Colour: Pink; White; Red; Violet; Purple; Blue; Varied
First Bloom: April
Amount of Sun Needed: Mild
Scent: None
Petal Size: Medium

25.Grape Hyacinth (Muscari)
Colour: Blue
First Bloom:
Amount of Sun Needed: Moderate to Full
Scent: None
Petal Size: Small(Bulb-like)

26.Grecian Windflower (Anemone Blanda)
Colour: Blue; Violet; White; Yellow(Centre)
First Bloom:
Amount of Sun Needed: Mild to Moderate
Scent: None
Petal Size: Fairly Medium

27.Hydrangea (Hydrangea)
 Colour: Blue; Pink; White; Red; Varied
First Bloom: May
Amount of Sun Needed: Moderate to Full
Scent: None
Petal Size: Small to Moderate

28. Huntington Carpet Rosemary (Rosmarinus officinalis)
    Colour: Light Blue; White
    First Bloom: April
    Amount of Sun Needed: Mild
    Scent: Mild
    Petal Size: Small

29. Iris 'Babbling Brook' – Tall Bearded (Iris germanica)
Colour: White; Sky Blue; Yellow
First Bloom: May
Amount of Sun Needed: Moderate to Full
Scent: None
Petal Size: Fairly Large

A source of inspiration for the traditional symbol of French royalty, irises have a stylised appearance of their petals that speaks of elegance and representation for the elite upper class. The combination of colours, like the stunning blue, white and yellow in these Iris **'Babbling Brook,' are particularly well-matched in hues that call for hopeful admiration and awe.**

30.Kalanchoe (Kalanchoe blossfeldiana)
Colour: Red; Pink; White; Varied
First Bloom: March
Amount of Sun Needed: Mild
Scent: None
Petal Size: Small

31."Leander" English Rose by David Austin (Rosa)
 Colour: Apricot; Light Peach; White
 First Bloom: June
 Amount of Sun Needed: Moderate to Full
 Scent: None
 Petal Size: Medium

A classic favourite for rose-lovers, Leander exudes refined beauty and noble stature with mild to deep colours and unique numerous petals of its flowers, a remarkable splendour of its class that enlightens and inspires…

32.Lily (Lilium)
Colour: White; Pink; Red; Yellow; Varied
First Bloom: Late April to Early May
Amount of Sun Needed: Moderate
Scent: Mild to Strong
Petal Size: Medium to Large

33.Lupine
Colour: Purple; Violet; Yellow; Green; Varied
First Bloom: May
Amount of Sun Needed: Full
Scent: Mild
Petal Size: Small to Fairly Medium

34.Marguerite Daisy (Argyranthemum frutescens)
Colour: White; Yellow; Orange; Varied
First Bloom: Late April to May
Amount of Sun Needed: Wide Range from Mild to Full
Scent: Minimal
Petal Size: Small to Moderate

35.Nemesia (Nemesia caerulea)
Colour: White; Light Pink; Light Blue; Purple; Yellow
First Bloom: April
Amount of Sun Needed: Moderate
Scent: None
Petal Size: Medium

36.Pansy (Viola tricolor var. hortensis)
Colour: Purple; Blue; Yellow; Orange; White; Varied
First Bloom: March
Amount of Sun Needed: Moderate
Scent: None
Petal Size: Small to Medium

37.Peach Blossom (Prunus persica)
    Colour: Yellow; Pink; Red; White
    First Bloom: February
    Amount of Sun Needed: Moderate to Full
    Scent: None
    Petal Size: Small

Originating from East Asia, the peach blossom flower is an early spring delight for the most significant cultural festive occasion of the year in the region. Symbolic and an inspiration for numerous legends, peach blossoms are ornamental favourites for both indoor and outdoor displays while the season is still mild, and winter cold has yet to fully end.

Agile evergreen leaves eagerly sprout from the sturdy branches of these peach blossom shoots amongst dainty soft pink flowers budding fervently, placed indoor for shelter and refuge from the late winter chills.

38.Petunia (Petunia)
Colour: Purple; Blue; Yellow; Pink; Varied
First Bloom: April
Amount of Sun Needed: Moderate to Full
Scent: None
Petal Size: Small to Medium

With dangling flower stalks and bright petals, petunias are often the foremost choice for hanging baskets.

39.Plum Blossom (Prunus Mume)
Colour: Red, Pink, White, Yellow(Stamen)
First Bloom: March
Amount of Sun Needed: Moderate to Full
Scent: Mild to Strong
Petal Size: Small to Medium

"Cherry Plum Blossom"

A glorious sunny weather and radiant blue sky in 2024 offer the perfect back-drop for this flourishing plum blossom in its peak bloom, an ageless classic within this city of nature pursuits.

40.Poppy (Papaver rhoeas)
Colour: Red, Pink, Black(centre)
First Bloom: June
Amount of Sun Needed: Moderate to Full
Scent: None
Petal Size: Fairly Large

A long-time symbol for veterans' Remembrance Day, red poppy flowers serve as a nice colour complement to other flower mix in public park gardens such as the Queen Elizabeth Rose Garden, as in the above.

41."Pretty Lady" Rose by Floribunda(Rosa)
Colour: Peach;Pink;White
First Bloom: June
Amount of Sun Needed:Mild to Moderate
Scent: None
Petal Size: Medium

42. Primrose (Primula vulgaris)
Colour: Blue; Purple; Yellow; Pink; Red; Orange; White; Varied
First Bloom: Late February
Amount of Sun Needed: Mild to Moderate
Scent: None
Petal Size: Medium

The first bloom of a colorful variety of Primrose in late February heralded the start of the 2019 flowering season in Vancouver as garden centres and shops began filling their shelves and display areas with these early blossoms of the year.

43."Rhapsody in Blue" Rose(Rosa)
Colour: Purple; Violet; Yellow(Stamen)
First Bloom: August
Amount of Sun Needed: Moderate to Full
Scent: None
Petal Size: Medium

44.Romantica Hybrid Tea Rose (Rosa 'Frederic Mistral')
    Colour: Shell Pink
    First Bloom: September
    Amount of Sun Needed: Mild to Moderate
    Scent: None
    Petal Size: Medium

45.Rose (Rosa)
    Colour: Varied
    First Bloom: Late Spring May to June
    Amount of Sun Needed: Moderate to Full
    Scent: Varied
    Petal Size: Varied

46.Rosa "Chinook Sunrise"
　　Colour: Soft Mixed Peach Yellow Orange
　　First Bloom: June
　　Amount of Sun Needed: Moderate to Full
　　Scent: None
　　Petal Size: Medium
　　An award-winning jewel of the country, "Chinook Sunrise" is simply a gentle reminder
and representative of the glows of sunrise, freshness upon earth and graciousness dawned.

47.Rosa "Golden Celebration" (English Rose Cultivar by David Austin)
    Colour: Golden Yellow
    First Bloom: June
    Amount of Sun Needed: Moderate to Full
    Scent: Mild
    Petal Size: Medium

True to its name, Rosa "Golden Celebration" celebrates the colour and energy of great occasions with cheer and liveliness of its heartwarming sight, a joyful companion to any gathering…

48.Royal Candle (Veronica spicata)
    Colour: Red
    First Bloom: May
    Amount of Sun Needed: Mild to Moderate
    Scent: None
    Petal Size: Small

49.Senetti (Pericallis x hybrida)
Colour: White; Light Purple; Blue; Pink; Yellow; Varied
First Bloom: May
Amount of Sun Needed: Moderate to Full
Scent: None
Petal Size: Medium

50.Shasta Daisy (Leucanthemum X superbum)
Colour: White: Golden Yellow(Centre)
First Bloom: June
Amount of Sun Needed: Mild to Full
Scent: Mild to Strong
Petal Size: Medium

51.Snapdragon (Antirrhinum majus)
Colour: Red; Yellow; Pink; White; Varied
First Bloom: May
Amount of Sun Needed: Moderate to Full
Scent: None
Petal Size: Medium

52.Tulip (Tulipa)
   Colour: Red; Yellow; Purple; Pink; White; Varied
   First Bloom: March
   Amount of Sun Needed: Moderate to Full
   Scent: None
   Petal Size: Medium to Fairly Large

53.Verbena a.k.a. Vervain
Colour: Purple; Violet
First Bloom: August-September
Amount of Sun Needed: Moderate to Full
Scent: None
Petal Size: Tiny

54.Virginia Spiderwort (Tradescantia virginiana)
Colour: Bluish Purple, Yellow
First Bloom: August
Amount of Sun Needed: Mild to Moderate
Scent: None
Petal Size: Small to Fairly Medium

55.Weigela(Weigela)
Colour: Red; Pink; White; Varied
First Bloom: May
Amount of Sun Needed: Mild
Scent: None
Petal Size: Small to Fairly Medium

56.Wisteria (Wisteria floribunda)
Colour: Purple; White; Yellow; Varied
First Bloom: May
Amount of Sun Needed: Moderate to Full
Scent: None
Petal Size: Small to Fairly Medium

Japanese purple Wisteria in its early stage of bloom.

57.Yarrow (Achillea millefolium)
Colour: White, Yellow
First Bloom: June
Amount of Sun Needed: Mild to Moderate
Scent: None
Petal Size: Considerably Small

58.Yellow Coneflower (Echinacea)
 Colour: Yellow, Dark Brown(Centre)
 First Bloom: August
 Amount of Sun Needed: Moderate
 Scent: None
 Petal Size: Medium

www.ingramcontent.com/pod-product-compliance
Lightning Source LLC
Chambersburg PA
CBHW041548120626
46551CB00002B/149